# OF COURSE I'M ANTI-

## AREN'T YO

# OF COURSE I'M ANTI-PSYCHIATRY.

# AREN'T YOU?

## AN ILLUSTRATED CRITIQUE OF 21ST CENTURY PSYCHIATRY

## AUNTIE PSYCHIATRY

momerath publishing

First published in Great Britain 2017

Momerath Publishing

ISBN 978-0-9573137-2-9

www.auntiepsychiatry.com

ap@auntiepsychiatry.com

# List of illustrations

1. Psychiatry is like an apple     3

2. Deconstructing the Royal College of Psychiatrists' logo     5

3. Debunking the Diabetes Analogy     7

4. Big Pharma Boogie     9

5. Top Trumps: Psychiatric Theories     11

6. Are Antidepressants Over-Prescribed?     13

7. Recovery Begins with Non-Compliance     17

8. It's the Sleep Deprivation, Stupid!     19

9. Let's Play 'Brain or Blame'     21

10. An Anti-Anti Stigma Campaign     23

11. On the Road to Little Torpid     25

12. Haldol is not a Fun Drug     27

13. The Right Prescription     29

14. Celebrating Crazy Talk     31

15. Snakes and Ladders: Escape from the Psych Ward     33

16. Exploring the Upside of Melancholia     35

17. Snakes on a Brain     38

18. Psychiatry is...     39

19. More Bang for your Butt     40

20. Arsey Psychic     41

21. Let Wisdom Guide     42

22. Dr Pies Stays Positive     43

23. Turning the Tables     44

24. Psy the Snake's Student Worksheet     45

25. Rigging Clinical Trials: Exam Paper     49

26. Schizophrenia: Looking for it in Genetix     51

27. Shill Doc Millionaire     53

28. Sir Simon: Defender of the Faith     55

29. For Garth     57

30. Microchip Meds     59

31. A Shared Moment of Insight     61

" OF COURSE i'M
ANti-PSychiAtRy.
ARen't you ? "

teD CHABASiNSKi

1. CRAzy tALK

### "Of course I'm anti-psychiatry. Aren't you?"

My transformation began with this challenge. It was served up by veteran human rights activist Ted Chabasinski in a blog post to the social justice website *Mad in America*. On the face of it, this challenge was not for me. I was a good-as-gold patient, grateful for the mental health services provided by my GP's surgery. I got along well with my psychiatric nurse and trusted her judgement, I sought out prescription psych-drugs and took them willingly, without coercion – how could I be anti-psychiatry?

But Ted's proposition would not leave me be, and here's why: I knew then, and I know now, that when psychiatry is bad, it is very, very bad. There is rot at the core of psychiatry.

### What is Psychiatry?

There are several major professional bodies of Psychiatry around the world. Perhaps the most influential is the American Psychiatric Association (APA). Here is the APA definition:

'Psychiatry is the branch of medicine focused on the diagnosis, treatment and prevention of mental, emotional and behavioral disorders.' *(www.psychiatry.org)*

This is the important bit: *Psychiatry is a branch of medicine.* Psychiatrists are top dogs, and they are trained to understand the human inner-world in *medical* terms. Psychiatry is the language of disease and diagnosis, medication and malfunctioning brain circuitry. This rattles down the Mental Health chain, finally settling into the received wisdom of societies all around the world.

### What does it mean to be anti-psychiatry?

Now there's a question! The answers are complex, deep-rooted and tricky to excavate – a job for a creature with an elongated snout, formidable fore-claws, fearsome spirit… and a fondness for honey ants. Step forward Auntie Psychiatry.

*The rot at the core of Psychiatry.* This was my first anti-psychiatry cartoon. The 'rotten at the core' analogy is one I've used for years. Developing the concept into a visual image was very rewarding. At this stage of my conversion to anti-psychiatry, I felt the need to be somewhat equivocal – I couldn't quite say that Psychiatry is *all* bad... but, well, you get the idea.

3

# Let Wisdom Guide

And so, I set forth in the guise of a giant anteater. First, I went in search of the imagery and symbolism chosen by Psychiatry to represent itself. A cursory Google search led me to the Royal College of Psychiatrists and its absurdly imperious logo.

The logo is comprised of many elements: snakes, butterflies, a medieval helmet and the ankh symbol to name but a few. After searching in vain for clues to the history of the logo and the significance of the symbolism, I e-mailed an enquiry to the College, and felt genuinely pleased to receive this enlightening reply from the 'Archivist and Record Manager':

"The College logo dates back to 1926 when the Coat of Arms were originally granted to the Royal Medico-Psychological Association, the predecessor body of the College. The logo incorporates the traditional caduceus and serpents symbolic of medicine. The traditional butterflies associated with psyche representing human soul or spirit because of its lightness and ephemeral life. The serpents representing wisdom and health, being associated with Aescupalius, the God of Medicine and with Hygeia the Goddess of Health – hence twined round Staff of Aescupalius. The looped cross, representing the Egyptian Cross (ANK) of Life, winged to signify life's transience."

Even at this larval stage as a novice and clumsy cartoonist, I could see that I'd struck satirist's gold. The 'serpents representing wisdom and health' may indeed be symbolic of medicine, but to the lay eye they appear hissing and venomous, arched and ready to strike. Is that really a good image for Psychiatry? Then there is the motto: LET WISDOM GUIDE. There'd be mileage in that, I was sure. And finally, the incumbent Mr President, Professor Sir Simon Wessely with his formidable string of mighty impressive letters after his name – MA, BM, BCh, MSc, MD, FRCP, FRCPsych, FMedSci FKC.

FKC?? Little help, anyone?

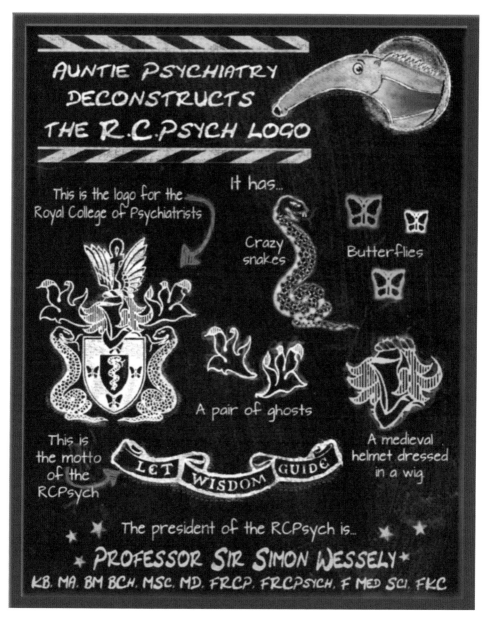

The Royal College is clearly very proud of this logo – it dominates the pavement outside their HQ, blown up to enormous proportions. Wonder how many of them stop to take a good look and think about the message it sends out? Two evil snakes jealously guarding their symbols of power and authority... Good call!

## Psychiatry's Fat Whoppers

If there is one thing Psychiatry excels at, it is suckering obliging charities, well-meaning campaigners, trusting journalists and amenable celebrities into spreading their fallacious memes. I have selected ten of the most shameless of these, and sprinkled them throughout the book to illustrate what is going on, starting with…

## Fat Whopper #1: The Diabetes Analogy

This particular Fat Whopper has been around for decades, and is a fiercely resistant strain. It is brought to us by Psychiatry's professional bodies and opinion leaders. Here's the American Psychiatric Association:

"Most medications are used by psychiatrists in much the same way that medications are used to treat high blood pressure or diabetes." *(www.psychiatry.org)*

The meme is then picked up and endorsed by follow-the-leader medics. Here's UCLA psychiatrist Dr Tom Strouse:

"People often believe that mental illness reflects moral weakness or lack of sufficient willpower – and that's false. Psychiatric illnesses are just as real as diabetes or high blood pressure." *(www.uclahealth.org 2016)*

Note the sham dichotomy: It's either 'moral weakness' or 'real illness.' Your choice. More on this later.

From there it finds fertile ground in the minds of Mental Health campaigners and media pawns. Here's Ruby Wax, OBE:

"You'll always get someone saying 'you don't need to take medication for depression, you just need to buck up.' Yeah? Are you going to take away a diabetic's insulin and tell them to buck up?" *(www.kingston.ac.uk 2016)*

Then it pops up all over – newspapers, chat shows, twitter, blogs, conversations at the bus-stop… The result? A decades long bumper toxic harvest for the Pharma Giants. Lovely-jubbly!

Depression, Schizophrenia, Bipolar Disorder – just about any diagnosis will do – it is 'one size fits all' with this particular Fat Whopper. I struggled to find an entertaining angle for this cartoon, and was about to give up when the image of a Seussville signpost came to mind. From that moment, everything fell into place, and the cartoon took on a life of its own.

## Big Pharma Boogie

**Marge:** "You know, Homer, it's very easy to criticize."

**Homer:** "Fun too."

Homer is right, it *is* fun to criticise, but there are times when I feel just a little guilty for taking a swipe at doctors who are doing their damnedest at the coalface. Here is Dr Andrew Green, senior General Practitioner, voicing his concerns about rising prescription rates for antidepressants in the UK.

"We don't act in isolation; we have guidance to help us. The guidance is explicit, and it might surprise you. In England, NICE is very clear. It says... 'provide antidepressants to those with moderate disease, continue for between 6 months and 2 years.' It also recommends antidepressants for patients with 'mild disease' in certain circumstances, even though it acknowledges lack of evidence for their use. If GPs deviate from guidelines they have to be able to show the reasons why. Many GPs are understandably anxious about explaining why they have deviated from guidance, to people like coroners."

Well, Dr Green, the guidance doesn't surprise me at all, not one iota, but you make a very powerful and important point – all health professionals have been co-opted by Psychiatry, and are forced to dance in lockstep to the same tune: The Big Pharma Boogie. And with this official advice on the NHS Choices website...

'Some people think depression is trivial and not a genuine health condition. They're wrong – it is a real illness with real symptoms. Depression isn't a sign of weakness or something you can 'snap out of' by 'pulling yourself together'.

It's important to seek help from your GP if you think you may be depressed. Many people wait a long time before seeking help for depression, but it's best not to delay. The sooner you see a doctor, the sooner you can be on the way to recovery.'

...you'll be helping to fill those Big Pharma coffers for many years to come. So, of *course* I'm anti-psychiatry. Aren't you?

When I look back at these early cartoons, I remember feeling a pressing need to get in all the relevant information and be super-accurate about it. The image of the NHS cash cow being milked dry by Big Pharma wasn't enough... I had to add the RC Psych guidelines underneath to back up my point. I like to think that as my cartooning skills developed, I became more adept at incorporating these vital components into the image itself... or did I just become less bothered?

# Fat Whopper #2: The Chemical Imbalance Theory

"Psychiatric medications can help correct imbalances in brain chemistry that are thought to be involved in some mental disorders" *(American Psychiatric Association)*

The 'Chemical Imbalance Theory', a natural companion to The Diabetes Analogy, is a real tough cookie. This catchy phrase with its sciency ring is a Pharma marketing dream. It was breathed into life by Psychiatry's opinion leaders, and thereafter spread like topsy, tripping off the tongues of mental health staff, GPs, newspaper columnists and anti-stigma campaigners for more than a generation, and still going strong. Here's Dr Joanna Moncrieff:

"I have heard many psychiatrists explain to patients that their symptoms are due to a chemical imbalance, that taking psychiatric medication is like taking insulin for diabetes, that the drugs will help rectify this chemical imbalance and that without the drugs the condition will rapidly recur." *(The Myth of the Chemical Cure, p.10)*

Despite Psychiatry's gung-ho insistence that the illnesses they treat are 'real', just like diabetes or heart disease, society in general is strangely squeamish about using words such as 'disease' and 'illness', preferring coy euphemisms: 'problem', 'difficulty', 'disorder', 'condition'. 'Mental health problem' is the current front runner. This sensitivity signifies an intuitive recognition that these are not diseases of the brain so much as the onslaught of life.

And yet, by carpet bombing the media with the memes... *'It's a chemical imbalance'* and *'Mental illness is an illness like any other'*, Psychiatry has successfully wormed its way into our minds. Try challenging someone who is wedded to the validity of their medical diagnosis, and you can be met with a very hostile reaction: "But my suffering is *real*, it's severe, it's out of my control... I really do have a *real* illness." And I get this. The suffering *is* real, it *is* severe, at times it *is* out of my control... and yes, it *is* physical. But does that make it a *medical* illness, in the same way as diabetes or heart disease? Not in my book. Read on.

10

Top Trumps was a popular game in the 1970s when I was a kid, although heaven alone knows why. Each game went on and on, boredom setting in long before anyone actually won. Creating this cartoon is about the most fun I've ever had with Top Trumps. Looking at it now, it appears kind of unfinished – I'm kicking myself for not paying more attention to those three glaringly blank cards.

## Fat Whopper #3: Psychotropic Drugs are Medications

It's easy to fall into the habit of using the word 'medication' when writing about the drugs typically used by Psychiatry, but I prefer the term **psychotropic drugs** (psych-drugs for short). Psychiatrist Dr Joanna Moncrieff explains:

"There is no fundamental distinction between drugs used for psychiatric purposes and other psychoactive drugs. They all act on the nervous system to produce a state of altered consciousness, a state that is distinct from the normal undrugged state." *(The Myth of the Chemical Cure p.14)*

In other words, psych-drugs do not act therapeutically to correct an underlying malfunction in the same way as insulin for diabetes… rather, they induce a state of atypical neural activity that would not arise in an undrugged brain.

### Listen Up!

This is important. The difference between therapeutic medications such as insulin to control blood glucose levels, and psychotropic drugs that disrupt brain activity, demolishes Psychiatry's claims for its pharmaceutical arsenal. The deceitful branding of psych-drugs as 'antidepressants', 'antipsychotics' and 'mood stabilizers' misleads people into believing they are disease-specific, but Psychiatry's scattergun approach to prescribing says otherwise.

That's not to say that psych-drugs are worthless. Anyone who has scanned the comments generated by a newspaper columnist or blogger who expresses misgivings about antidepressants will inevitably come across a version of this:

"But Prozac saved my *LIFE!!!!*"

I'm never quite sure what this means, it could be any number of things, but this much I know: When a psych-drug feels like a life-saver, Beware! It may fix the pain, but it will not heal your brain.

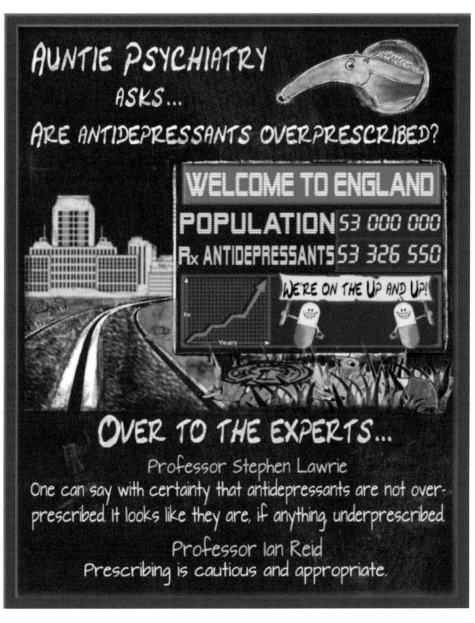

Are 'antidepressants' over-prescribed? With the 2015 Rx figure for England rising to **61 million**, hollow laughter all round from everyone in their right mind. And yet several lead psychiatrists assert with conviction that they are, if anything, *under-*prescribed. Now, I wonder why on earth they'd say *that*? This cartoon of a degraded, litter-strewn landscape contrasting with the neon billboard 'happy pills', didn't quite achieve the desolate atmosphere I had in mind. Still, the grinning pills are a triumph!

# RECOVERY BEGINS WITH NON-COMPLIANCE.

MAD MOVEMENT SLOGAN

2. MAD PRIDE

## Non-compliance is a state of mind

Psychiatry takes a dim view of non-compliance. While the surface sign of non-compliance is often 'medication non-adherence', this battle of wills about taking the drugs reveals something far more elemental: an urge to reassert autonomy, to fight for self-determination, to kick against the powers-that-be. As a consequence, Mental Health workers become expert at sniffing out the slightest whiff of rebellion. The savviest amongst them know how to work with this, seeing non-compliance as a *good* thing, a *healthy* act of human resistance. Such a response is rare.

## Mother Madness

My own conversion to non-compliance came when I discovered anti-psychiatry activism on the nascent Internet in 1995. It was through this band of early freedom fighters that I first heard the slogan *'Recovery begins with non-compliance'*. A revelation. Until that moment, I hadn't thought to question the medical line that I was doomed to a life of incurable and progressive brain disease.

I will be forever grateful to 'Mother Madness', Sylvia Caras, for helping me to turn my life around. In the early 90s, Sylvia had the insight, skills and tenacity to found the e-community 'Madness' – a safe space for *'people who experience mood swings, fear, voices and visions.'* I felt as though I had come home.

## Warning: Do not abruptly stop psychiatric drugs!

If you are thinking of going down the rebel route, don't chuck out your drugs just yet: going cold turkey is a massive no-no. Here's Peter Breggin, a rebel psychiatrist whose judgement I trust:

"Most psychiatric drugs are far more dangerous to take than people realise, but they also can become dangerous when discontinued too abruptly. Stopping psychiatric drugs should usually be done gradually, and only with professional guidance." *(Toxic Psychiatry 1993)*

AUNTIE PSYCHIATRY SAYS... RECOVERY BEGINS WITH NON-COMPLIANCE

LET WISDOM GUID

Depixol

Celexa

Schizophrenia patients taking regular antipsychotic medication over a 20 year study suffered MORE PSYCHOSIS, ANXIETY and COGNITIVE IMPAIRMENT than those who quit antipsychotic medication.

Harrow et al, Psychol Med. Oct 2012

The psych-ward drug round: which patient hasn't had fantasies about trashing that ridiculous altar? Psychiatry's ritual administration of medication to the line of patients, cowed and acquiescent, has always been a cornerstone of ward life. For this cartoon, I dressed the drug trolley with Psychiatry's holy symbolism – the Ankh from the RC Psych logo takes the place of a cross, jealously guarded by their venomous 'Serpent of Wisdom'.

## It's the sleep deprivation, stupid!

When it comes to manic psychosis, sleep deprivation provides the biggest, brightest red flag there is. Ask anyone who is on the road to psychosis how they are sleeping and you won't hear this: "Yeah, really well, like a baby." The script writers of Men in Black get it:

**Jay:** "Zed, don't you guys ever get any sleep around here?"

**Zed:** "The twins keep us on Centaurian time, standard thirty-seven hour day. Give it a few months. You'll get used to it... or you'll have a psychotic episode." *(MiB 1997)*

Novelist Adrian Barnes gets it… "After six days of absolute sleep deprivation, psychosis will set in" *(Nod 2012)*. Joe Public gets it… "Lack of sleep can make you crazy." But Psychiatry? Not so much.

The first time I found myself hurtling towards full-blown psychosis, a psych-doc told me this: "Don't sleep during the day!"

*Worst advice ever!*

## Keeping manic psychosis in check: This much I know.

- Natural sleep is everything. Day or night, it is sacrosanct.
- Drugged sleep is better than no sleep at all. But beware!
- Zopiclone at night is my drug of choice. Blissful oblivion. This in itself makes it dangerous.
- Withdrawal from Zopiclone causes severe REM rebound. Steel yourself against the nightmares, and be sure to taper.

Before you say it, yes, I know: the sleep deprivation of manic psychosis is not the same as common insomnia. It has an entirely different quality and trajectory. I can tell the difference after just one night. Whereas ordinary insomnia leaves me feeling drained and shitty, manic insomnia feeds the brewing supercell of creative energy, elation, terror, paranoia, disintegration. The cure, however, is the same: sweet, elusive, drug-free sleep.

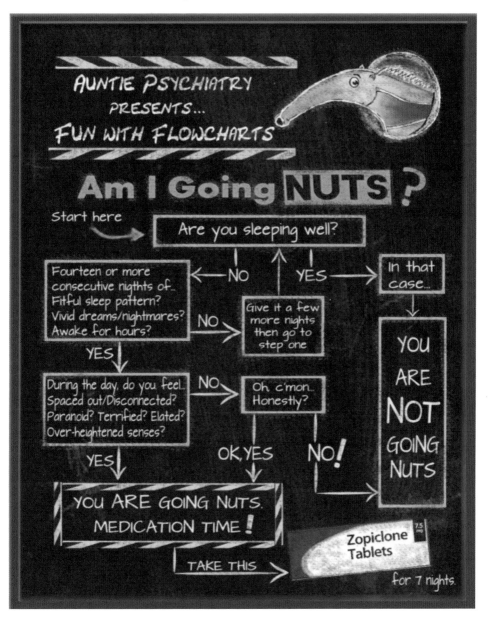

Looking at this again, I'd say the 'fourteen or more consecutive nights' is probably pushing it a bit. My psych-nurse suggests three nights, but that's way too cautious. Experience tells me that even a fairly prolonged run of sleepless nights can resolve itself naturally, and resorting to Zopiclone too soon is a mistake.

## Let's Play 'Brain or Blame'

Psychiatry has been playing this game for decades, using subtle and not-so-subtle tactics to signpost us all in the direction of BRAIN. Try typing the word *Psychiatry* into Google Images and see what comes up. Or check out the website of 'MQ', the *'new major mental health research charity'*. This charity's slick infomercial – 'MQ's Story' – features a man sitting in a busy hospital clinic, gingerly cradling his own brain in his lap. He waits in vain to be called – then the day ends, the lights go out and he is plunged into darkness. Poor guy! But hold on a moment... just when you think that all is lost, the dingy waiting room disappears, and he finds himself magically transported to a vibrant, hi-tech Wonderland. Around him the room bustles with bright, young staff in white coats busily engaged in all manner of impressive brain-related scientific projects. The guy in the waiting room chair hasn't moved an inch – he sits there all the while, carefully holding his exposed brain – but now he has hope that science will be his saviour... and he smiles.

## So...Your Choice: Brain or Blame?

"BLAME": You chose *blame??* Well, OK. It comes in two main flavours: self-blame (you're weak, contemptible, deplorable), or blaming others (they fuck you up). Mix and match for a lifetime of shame, guilt, reproach, alienation and recrimination. Psychiatry has the power to absolve you... Want to choose again?

"OK, BRAIN": The root cause of your craziness is 'malfunctioning brain circuitry'. All those crazy thoughts, overwhelming emotions and self-destructive behaviour – that's not *you*, it's your defective brain. No-one is to blame, nothing has to change, and you are not accountable for the activity of your afflicted brain. What's the catch? No-one is to blame, nothing has to change, and you are not accountable for the activity of your afflicted brain. Like the helpless guy in the waiting room chair, you are dependent and powerless.

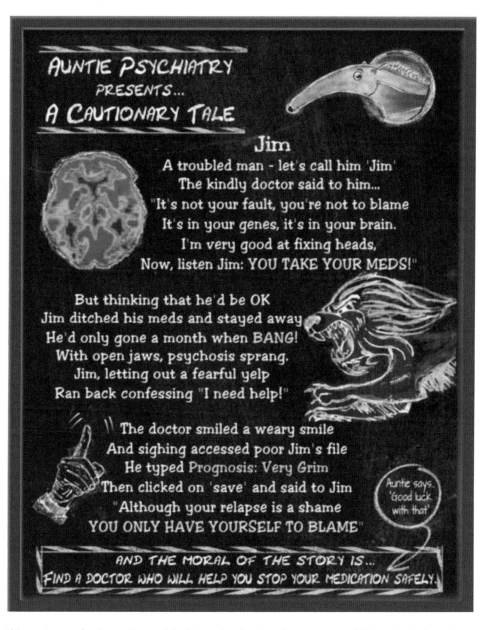

'It's not your fault, you're not to blame'... just so long as you follow doctor's orders. And don't get *too* dependent or demanding or you'll be condemned as attention-seeking and manipulative. This cautionary tale is a parody of: '*Jim: Who ran away from his nurse and was eaten by a lion*' by Hilaire Belloc. I loved this poem as a child, but I was never convinced by the moral *"always keep a-hold of nurse, for fear of finding something worse."* I mean, he is **EATEN** by a **LION**! How cool is **THAT**??

## Fat Whopper #4: Anti-stigma campaigns reduce stigma

I've always been wary of anti-stigma campaigns, but never pinned down quite why that should be. After all, more openness and communication is surely a good thing, encouraging connection and breaking down barriers... so what's that shudder I feel whenever Stephen Fry, Ruby Wax or Alistair Campbell start with the anti-stigma soapbox lectures?

Then I came across an excellent blog post by Sera Davidow. *False Arguments Part 2: Anti-anti-stigma*. Sera's words helped me to understand that the chill-down-my-spine effect was, in fact, caused by Psychiatry's *'illness like any other'* mantra, picked up and parroted by these celebs on a mission to 'stop the stigma'.

Sera writes: "the idea of developing and then promoting a solely medicalized way of understanding our distress is creating the very 'stigma' it seeks to eliminate." She describes the process memorably as a merry-go-round spinning at breakneck speed. That worked for me, but rather than a merry-go-round, which is fun and exciting, I pictured a lethal circular saw blade spinning faster and faster out of control.

## Stigma arises when mental pain is recast as medical illness

I'm quite sure that Psychiatry would turn purple with rage and indignation at the suggestion that diagnosis comes with the subtext: **Your inner self is diseased**. But isn't that the implication? I certainly felt that way in the bad old days when I placidly accepted that I was ill for life. The impossibility of separating my 'self' from the 'disease' brought about the most crippling despair. What would be the point in fighting? I'd be fighting myself, and what is more, I had already lost. My only hope lay in the expertise and pharmaceutical armoury of the medical profession... and I was fast beginning to realise that was no hope at all. There had to be another way.

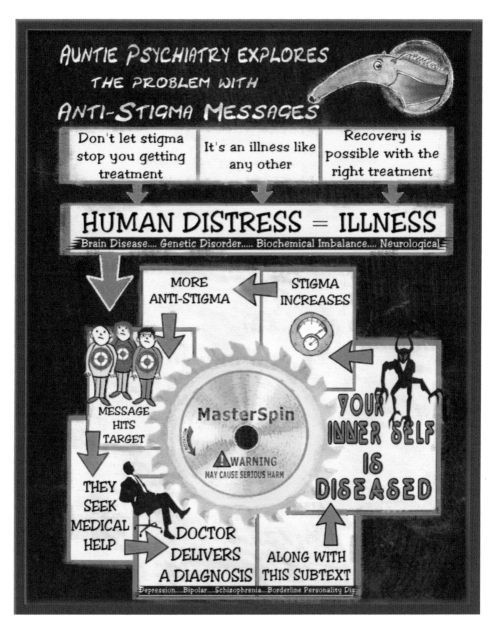

This one gave me some grief. My original idea was a rambling steampunk anti-stigma machine designed to spew out pots of lucre for Big Pharma because that's what it's ultimately all about. That plan fell by the wayside as the complexity of the workings got the better of me, and it morphed into this diagrammatic version. Looking at this cartoon now, my biggest regret is that the saw blade appears to be static. Oh well. I suppose it makes the warning on the disc blade readable.

## On the road to Little Torpid

*Which Way?* captures the allure of extreme inner states that can lead to psychosis. Anyone who has ever experienced full blown psychosis knows to their bitter cost that it is foolish and dangerous to stray from the sanity path – and yet, and yet – whenever a fork in the road appears, the 'pull' in that direction is very hard to resist.

Psychiatry strictly disapproves of flirting with the Danger Zone. It is interpreted as 'lack of insight' into your illness and noted down as yet another symptom of an underlying brain disease. The 'illness like any other' approach leaves absolutely no room for discovering spiritual meaning or fulfilment in these profound experiences.

Just after finishing 'Which Way?' I read the autobiography of neurologist Oliver Sacks in which he describes his brother Michael's lifelong struggle with 'schizophrenic' overwhelm. Here's a summary:

"Michael felt the psychosis had opened his eyes to things he had never previously thought about. On medication, he lost the sharpness and clarity with which he had perceived the world; everything seemed muffled – 'it's like being softly killed' he concluded. He called the non-schizophrenic world 'Rottenly Normal' – great rage was embodied in this incisive phrase." *(On the Move, Oliver Sacks, 2015)*

## Art as trigger factor

Creating this cartoon drove me a little bit crazy. The tree is *Forest Giant*, a magnificent seventeenth-century oak in the Forest of Dean. Happy memories of sitting beneath Forest Giant came back to me when I was searching for the perfect lure away from Little Torpid for my cartoon alter ego, but I struggled to convey the majestic beauty and benign solid presence of Forest Giant. It was only once I'd finished the cartoon that I realised that the monster in the woods can't be seen by my alter ego, who is, instead, transfixed by something that is just off the edge of the picture.

Which way? Oh, c'mon!

See the face in the tree smiling beatifically down? This is an example of *pareidolia*, a type of illusion which occurs when a random pattern is perceived as something meaningful. In this case, the accidental image was created by the light shining onto the stump of a dead branch. It puts me in mind of the tree-angels seen by the artist and visionary William Blake. I quote his words often: *'The tree which moves some to tears of joy is in the eyes of others only a green thing that stands in the way'*.

**"Haldol is not a fun drug."**

By hook or by crook, I have managed to avoid psych-docs for over twenty years, but every now and then I need something that only a doctor can provide – Zopiclone, Valium. Running the gauntlet of a visit to the GP at a time when my sense of self is disintegrating to the point of no return is not a piece of cake. The trick is to get a prescription for the drug I'm after without attracting too much attention, which means 'acting normal'. It's a lot like trying to appear sober when you're a bit squiffy – you're not kidding anyone.

Every fruitcake knows that maintaining eye contact with the doctor is the key to appearing sane, but this is the first thing to go. And even if you manage it for a few seconds, you are acutely aware that your eyes are a dead giveaway, a portal through which your inner turbulence is hideously exposed. And then there's controlling your body language, appearing attentive, pitching your voice to sound open and honest so that you give the impression that you're not 'holding out' even though you know damn well you are.

By and large, GPs are amenable to printing off a script and seeing you on your way… and nowadays, with a computer in every consulting room, even the eye contact thing can go unnoticed.

Once, a GP made a half-hearted attempt to persuade me to consider long-term antipsychotic 'maintenance' treatment. He handed me a script for a month's supply of Haldol, the drug I had been obliged to take in hospital.

Uh-uh, not going to happen. I was adamant.

He looked at me doubtfully for a long moment, then had the good grace to say, "OK, I'll admit, Haldol is not a fun drug." He didn't push it further.

Bless you, Dr Rodgers!

This cartoon went through a few transmutations before settling into this strange scene. My original idea was of a snake oil salesman (Pharm Rep) setting out his stall of 'good for everything that ails you' remedies, but the image didn't quite illustrate the point I was struggling to get across. There has been a definite mission creep in the sale of 'antipsychotics' in recent years – age and diagnosis no object – and if you don't like the first one, there are plenty more to try.

## The Right Prescription

Blagging sporadic prescriptions from uninterested GPs worked out fine for years. Then one day in 2008, an attentive GP looked at my notes, and he looked at me, and made an urgent phone call. He didn't tell me who he was phoning. I squirmed as I was forced to listen in to the animated conversation he was having about me with the person at the other end. Good god! He really saw me as batshit crazy! Eyeing the door, I considered doing a runner. But isn't that exactly what a batshit crazy bitch would do? He finished the call, and sounded pleased as he told me the good news: he'd arranged for me to see a member of the Community Mental Health Team later that day.

"I don't think so," I said evenly.

"No, no – trust me," he said, flapping his hands urgently, "it's difficult for you, I know, but I give you my word – you won't be sectioned. This is really important. You need someone to talk to."

And at last I made eye contact... and I *did* trust him.

The appointment was with the community psychiatric nurse (CPN). Skilled at helping me feel in control, I didn't need her often, not even once a year, but it was good to know she was there.

Once, she made a half-hearted attempt to persuade me to consider long-term antipsychotic maintenance treatment. "The newer drugs are a lot better," she said, "the side effects aren't nearly so bad." I nodded soberly and told her I'd give it some thought.

In June 2016 I received a letter from my psych nurse. She was writing to let me know that she had retired, and that the surgery would not be appointing a replacement CPN.

So... this gossamer safety net has been taken away. Back to blagging sporadic prescriptions from uninterested GPs.

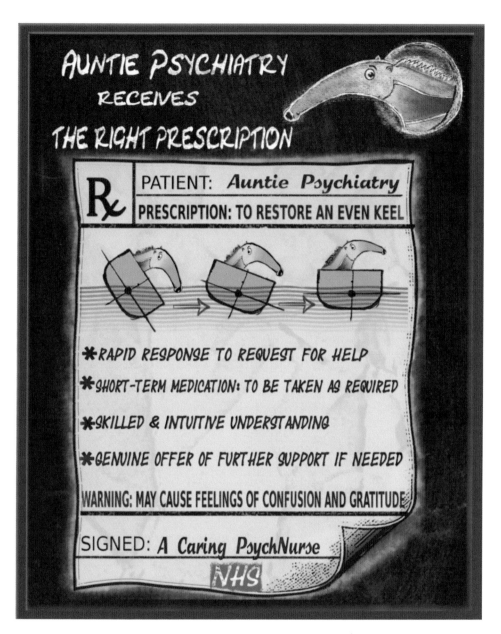

# AUNTIE PSYCHIATRY
### RECEIVES
## THE RIGHT PRESCRIPTION

**R** PATIENT: *Auntie Psychiatry*

PRESCRIPTION: TO RESTORE AN EVEN KEEL

＊RAPID RESPONSE TO REQUEST FOR HELP

＊SHORT-TERM MEDICATION: TO BE TAKEN AS REQUIRED

＊SKILLED & INTUITIVE UNDERSTANDING

＊GENUINE OFFER OF FURTHER SUPPORT IF NEEDED

WARNING: MAY CAUSE FEELINGS OF CONFUSION AND GRATITUDE

SIGNED: *A Caring PsychNurse*

NHS

This might seem an odd cartoon for an anti-psychiatry blog, but it represents my own experience of NHS mental health services in 2015. The technical sketch of the boat is a simplified version of a ship stability diagram. These generally show an outline of an empty vessel, but that seemed a little unfinished for this cartoon – the boat needed an occupant. Auntie climbed aboard, and her wavering emotions are written all over her face... although her expression doesn't change at all.

## Fat Whopper #5: Psychiatric Diagnoses are not Stigmatising

For this cartoon, I put together a small selection of the colourful words and phrases for madness that we all use from time to time. I love them; partly because they are so alive and vivid, but mostly because they bridge the scary gap between sanity and madness. Everyone can relate to being 'a bit bonkers' or 'away with the fairies' – these peppy colloquialisms are a great leveller.

Why is our language so rich with these lively expressions? My guess is that it's because they portray mental states we are fascinated by – scary, yes, but also mystical, alluring, exhilarating. Contrast this with the deadening language of Psychiatry. Worried about the offence that might be caused by these casual expressions, the UK anti-stigma charity 'Time to Change' provides a helpful *Mental Health Language Guide* to put us all straight. So instead of using words like mad, lunatic or unhinged, they suggest 'a person with a mental health problem' or 'someone who has a diagnosis of schizophrenia.' Yeah, whatever.

### Diagnosis dodging

It can be surprisingly difficult to get a straight answer to questions about diagnosis from Mental Health staff. When I asked my psych-nurse if I had an official diagnosis, she grimaced. "I don't think you'd find those labels terribly useful," she said, "but I can refer you to the psychiatrist for a definitive diagnosis if you feel it would help you." I told her I'd pass.

It strikes me as telling that the word 'label' so readily slips in to replace 'diagnosis' in this branch of medicine. Had we been talking about suspected diabetes, then of *course* I would want a definitive diagnosis, but to seek out a 'label' from Psychiatry? Give over! Here's the difference: Once it's been stuck on you, that label will haunt you like malignant shadow for the rest of your born days. Want to shake off stigma? Ditch your diagnosis.

Intending them to be carefree and playful, I sketched the fairies with big smiles, and was a little taken aback by the effect: decidedly mischievous and sinister. Here's a thought: I bet you can add a dozen more phrases for madness to my list... but how many everyday expressions do you know for diabetes?

# "A Strange Game. The Only Winning Move is Not to Play."

Despite vocal claims from Psychiatry that Psych beds are always, always in huge demand, once you have been admitted to a Psych ward, you can have a devil of a job persuading the powers-that-be to let you out again. Even if you went in there as a voluntary patient and can, in theory, simply walk off the ward, you just try it and see what happens. The mere threat of sectioning is enough to make most patients quickly think better of it.

The UK campaign group Speak Out Against Psychiatry (SOAP) identifies three main methods of escape:

1. The Runner
2. Play the Game
3. The Tribunal

By far the most successful of these is Method 2: Play the Game. It has been a long time since I was on a psych ward, and I was shocked to find out that the rules of the game haven't changed at all. The main difference seems to be that wards are now more 'secure', severely restricting your chances of Method 1: The Runner.

If you've never been a patient on a Psych ward, Auntie's Snakes and Ladders will give you some idea of how the game is played. You must convincingly feign compliance, insight and acquiescence. You soon learn that taking your meds is a Big Deal, and that it must be done willingly, without any resistance. Questioning your diagnosis is a no-no, as doing so implies 'Lack of Insight' into your illness. Other game tactics include: Never Joke with your Psychiatrist – they are notoriously humourless – and Don't Be A Smart Ass.

Once they let you go, the words of WOPR from the 1983 film War Games should be your guide: The only winning move is not to play.

I think I've had more comments about this cartoon than any other. Intended as an illustration of the absurdities faced by a patient on a psych ward, it turns out that some people try to make sense of it as a real board game. I guess it could be adapted into a real board game – 'You're Sectioned: Miss Three Turns', and 'Depot Injection: Go Back To Square One,' – that sort of thing. It could make a half-decent training aid for students. Any takers?

## Fat Whopper #6: Neuroimaging as clincher: The illness is 'real'

One of the most insidious aspects of modern Psychiatry is just how easily it has managed to manipulate a whole population's sense of self. All those messy, disturbing aspects of the human condition - agonising despair, wretched melancholy, unbearable heartache, anguish and torment - are stripped of their personal context, codified into a specious clinical diagnosis, and then treated as nothing more than malfunctioning brain circuitry. Here's an extract from Dr Mary-Ellen Lynall's blog for the 'The BMJ Opinion' (2016)

"Tomorrow's psychiatric trainee might show a video of a functional MRI scan to explain the malfunctioning circuitry in depression. For patients, carers, and families, being able to see and understand the physical changes underlying mental disorder and recovery could help to combat the stigma around mental health."

This neuro-vision is so very seductive, but does it hold water? Take a closer look and you'll see the clever artifice. Here's how it works. 1) Start by asserting the cast-iron conviction that depression is a medical illness caused by 'malfunctioning circuitry'. 2) Scan the patient's brain to reveal the colourful blobs of activity. 3) Play 'spot the difference' with a control brain. Ta-dah! The depression is made manifest. 4) Claim this to be incontrovertible evidence for point 1.

Such circular reasoning is classic Psychiatry. fMRI scans are fascinating, and I'm pretty sure my own brain would perform beautifully in showing the typical brain signatures during my darkest times, but how would that help me? Over the years, I have got to know my depression, and devised my own tactics for escaping its clutches. Strip away the human context by reframing it as pathological, and the Hell becomes unfathomable. Final words go to Dr Philip Hickey, who captures my experience perfectly with this:

"Depression, either mild or severe, transient or lasting, is not a pathological condition. It is the **natural, appropriate, and adaptive response** when a feeling-capable organism confronts an adverse event or circumstance."

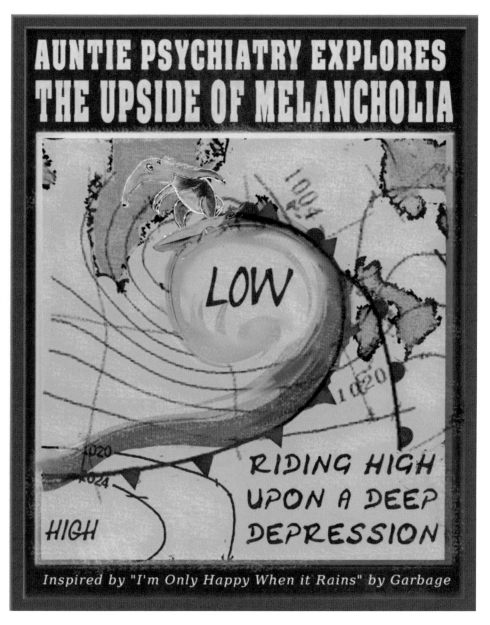

# AUNTIE PSYCHIATRY EXPLORES THE UPSIDE OF MELANCHOLIA

LOW

RIDING HIGH UPON A DEEP DEPRESSION

HIGH

*Inspired by "I'm Only Happy When it Rains" by Garbage*

*"Melancholy is as seductive as ecstasy."* This quote by Mason Cooley illustrates a side to depression that very few people these days are prepared to acknowledge. Society *used* to get it... before Psychiatry and Big Pharma muscled in to tilt our collective perception towards brain disease. But the valuable insight clings on: This cartoon is inspired by the Garbage track, *'I'm Only Happy When It Rains'*. Go on, find it now on YouTube... and crank up the volume. Knocks spots off Seroxat.

"THE
PROCESSION
MUSt
GO ON"

tHE NAKED EMPEROR

3.IN tHE AltOGEtHER

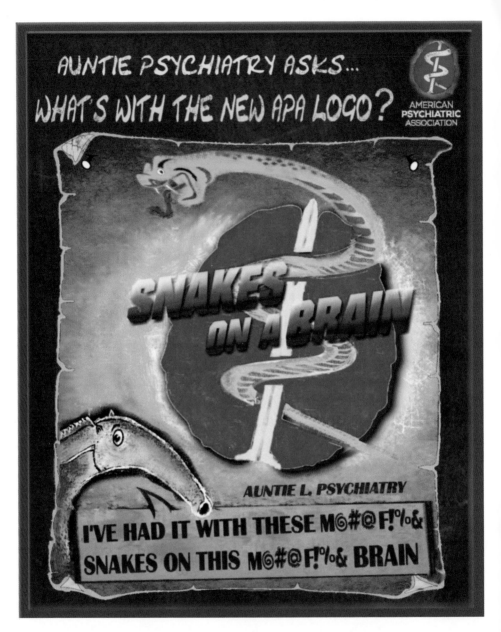

I had a great time creating this spoof *Snakes on a Plane* movie poster. The joke got even better when I discovered Samuel L Jackson's classic line... **"Enough is enough! I've had it with these m@#!F%'& snakes on this m@#!F%'& plane!"** Only trouble is... I made the rebranded APA logo look cool. Dammit! Many thanks to Dr Phil Hickey for planting the idea for this cartoon with his excellent blog post: 'The APA's New Image.'

This is the one and only cartoon for which I had a very clear idea of how the end picture would look, and it worked out exactly as I envisaged. Well, not *quite* exactly… I hadn't seen the Escher desk toy with its wandering ants, but once I'd put together the computer screen and keyboard, I felt the desktop lacked a certain something. The results of the Google Autocomplete game are pretty consistent – I've just tried it now, and got the same list. You can decide for yourself what that might imply.

I was brought up in a dairy farming family, and my dad subscribed to the magazine, **Farmers Weekly**. Its glossy, yellow/red cover came back to me as I was pondering cartoon ideas for Invega Trinza, the antipsychotic mega-injection. The spoof title 'Pharma's Weekly' was obvious... but what about the headline? Of course! **More Bang for your Butt!** Can't believe Janssen didn't get there first.

40

When I heard about the 2016 gathering of Psychiatrists at the RC Psych International Congress, I knew this venerable occasion was ripe for satire. But how? The lightbulb moment came when I discovered the College's very own event hashtag: #RCPsychIC. Arsey Psychic! What a gift! From that moment, all the cards fell into place. It proved to be the most satisfying cartoon to create, and I am very happy with the end result – the neon show-sign still makes me smile.

This cartoon was born of an upwelling of deeply suppressed rage at the reckless, dogmatic and greedy practice of psychiatrists across history that continues to this day – all in the name of 'patient care.' The 1994 film 'The Mask', made a big impression on me at the time, and the harum-scarum antics of Jim Carrey came back when I was mulling ideas for this cartoon. To this day, the Psnakes of Psychiatry can't resist the lure of The Mask that brings power. Let Wisdom Guide.

I've long been a fan of The Devil's Dictionary, and the definition of 'positive' is one of my favourites. We've all been 'positive' from time to time – be honest – but none so loudly, or publicly or repeatedly as Ronald W. Pies MD. Despite a mountain of evidence to the contrary, Dr Pies remains adamant that Psychiatry never bought into the "chemical imbalance theory" of mental illness, and continues to claim that his profession does not and hasn't ever promoted it to the public. Go figure.

AUNTIE PSYCHIATRY TURNS THE TABLES

This cartoon was inspired by a Mad in America blog post: 'Physician, Heal Thyself' by Daniel Kriegman, and features Psychiatry Psnakes 'tonguing and spitting out the bitter pill of reality'. It took quite a bit of working out. I had fun picturing the Psnakes being forced to queue at the trolley for their 'treatment', and I was surprised and pleased by the claustrophobic atmosphere of that room. Dan is optimistic that "in the end they will have to swallow the bitter pill and face reality." Here's hoping.

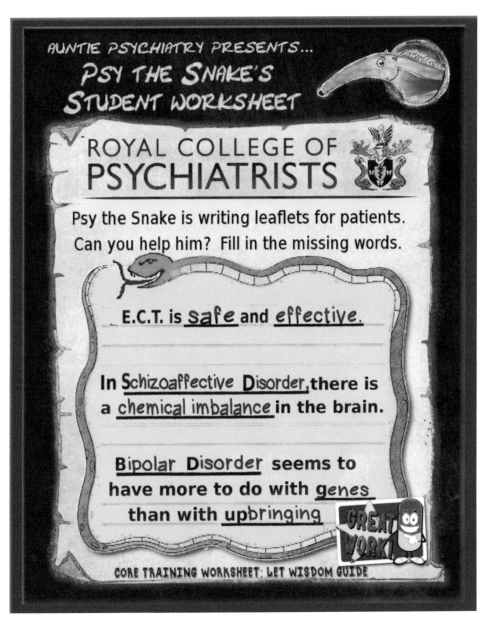

Here I pick up on the advice and information presented to patients and carers in leaflets published by the Royal College of Psychiatrists. According to the RCPsych website, 'each leaflet/factsheet reflects the best evidence base at the time of writing.' If I have a least favourite cartoon, this is it. The creative process for most of the others was challenging but fun, sometimes exhilarating, but this one just never felt right somehow. The best bit was making the 'reward sticker'. Great work!

45

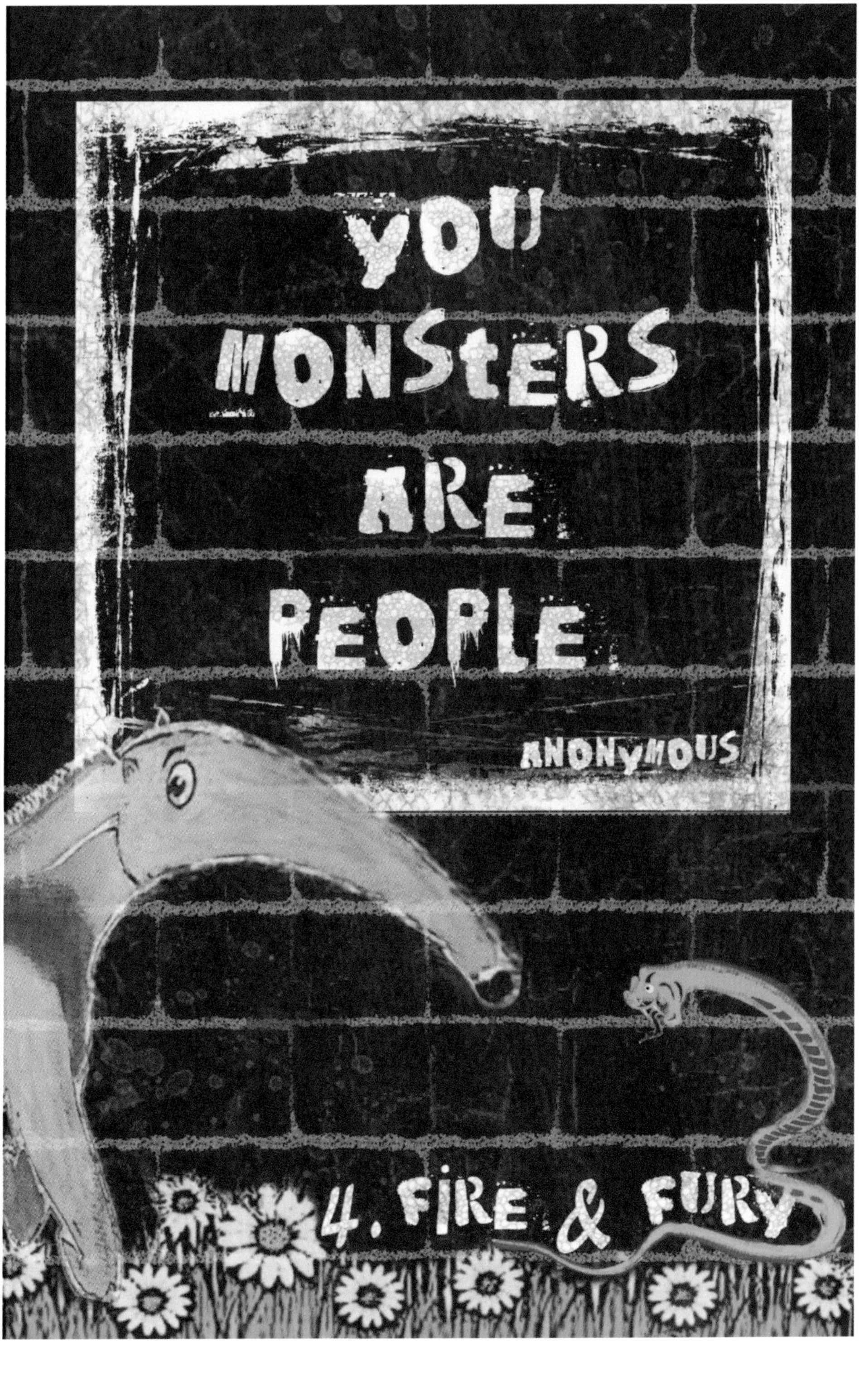
YOU MONSTERS ARE PEOPLE
ANONYMOUS
4. FIRE & FURY

## Fat Whopper #7: Psych-drugs are rigorously tested

As an undergraduate in the late 1980s, I picked up a skill that would prove its worth in later life: Critical Appraisal of the Scientific Literature. I learnt to assess papers for things like; strength of the design, validity of the research method, and the soundness of the authors' conclusions. I soon discovered that no paper was perfect – there would always be a weakness to probe, a loose thread to pull – but the one thing I never encountered was naked trickery.

And so, to this cartoon. The inspiration was prompted by a Pharma backed 'randomized clinical trial' for an injectable antipsychotic. Published in *JAMA Psychiatry (2015)*, a heavyweight, peer-reviewed medical journal, the trial was carefully designed to bring about the best possible outcome for the drug company. It required the co-operation of doctors to ensure that *ALL* the subjects had been administered the drug for many months. The drug was then abruptly withdrawn from those randomly allocated to the placebo group – there was no tapering phase, no additional support.

I was staggered by the audacity of this ruse. The American Psychiatric Association's own official guidance is unequivocal: 'medications should **never** be stopped abruptly as rebound psychosis may result': And this information has actually been incorporated into the trial design to maximise the risk of relapse in the placebo group. Something else!

I was beginning to detect a funny smell. If Psychiatry had made it so easy for a Pharma Giant to get away with this one, what other tricks were they getting up to? Digging around, it didn't take me long to locate the source of the smell – the stinking, rotten underbelly of the psych-drug trials racket. Psychiatry and Big Pharma have been in cahoots for decades, exploiting patients as expendable pawns to keep their monstrous, putrid psych-drug gravy train hurtling down the tracks. Don't believe me? Try digging yourself. You'll see.

This is a fictitious (yet scarily plausible) exam paper for *Rigging Clinical Trials*. The student has found a creative way to present the answer, but looking at it now, I realise that it appears as though ALL the placebo group fall prey to the sharks, and ALL of the drug group stay high and dry. In fact, there were patients in the placebo group who did not relapse into psychosis, and patients in the drug group who did. I'm not quite sure how to portray that in a simple cartoon though. Any ideas?

## Fat Whopper #8: A genetic breakthrough is around the corner

Does schizophrenia really have a 'significant genetic component' as is so often claimed? All of the evidence so far (and there's a hell of a stack of it) points in the same direction... NOPE!

But that isn't going to stop the frenzied Woozle hunt, not likely. Backed by a tsunami of ready money, research institutes and universities are racing to be the first to bag their trophy. No wonder the headlines keep springing up like toadstools after a warm shower of rain. Try typing *Schizophrenia Genes* into Google, restricting the search to Past Month, and see what appears. Tell you what, I'll save you the bother... *Breakthrough discovery, New insights, Step towards a real diagnostic test, Hope for future drug treatments.* All bullshit... and the biggest bullshit of all: *End to Stigma.*

Such press releases are catnip to journalists. The result? Well, we all know that 'mental illness is genetic', don't we? Nice one, Psychiatry.

## Occam's Razor

Don't get me wrong - I'm fascinated by the fields of genetics and neuroscience. Anti-psychiatry activists are often accused of being anti-science, but that's not true at all. Take this project, led by Dr Sergiu Pasca of Stanford University...

'By taking stem cells from people with schizophrenia who have specific genetic mutations, the team can create tiny 'minibrains' – each smaller than a pea – that emulate parts of a foetal human brain.' *(www.mqmentalhealth.org 2017)*

Genetically engineered brains no bigger than a pea? That's fantastic! But as enticed as I am by this vision, I have a sneaking suspicion that all the useful leads are hiding in plain, mundane sight. Abuse and neglect in infancy, bullying, bereavement, drugs, spiralling debt, homelessness... any more for any more? Finding a cure to all of that is a lot to expect from a lab full of minibrains.

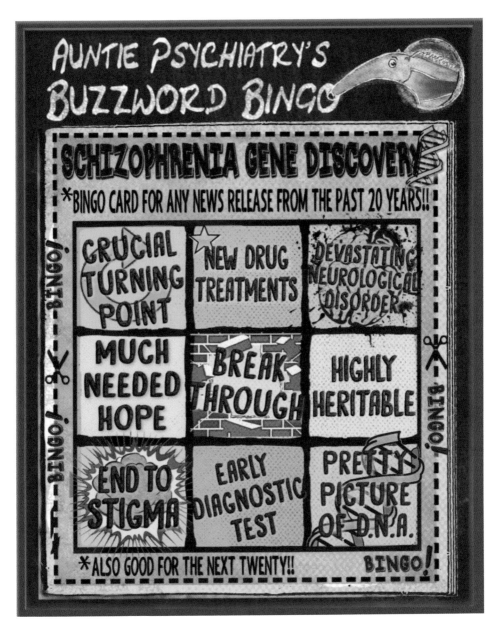

This was fun to do. It took no time at all to find nine recurring claims over the past 20-odd years of genetic research to fill the grid – there were more, but for the sake of clarity I limited it to nine. The Bingo card gives a good snapshot view of how 'schizophrenia' looks to scientists – a devastating brain disease in desperate need of a cure. The cause and the cure are always tantalisingly within reach, like the end of a rainbow, just give it a *little* more time, a *little* more money…

51

# Fat Whopper #9: Antipsychotic drugs protect the brain

"Psychiatry is not easily swayed by scientific evidence." *(Peter Breggin, 1993)*

This cartoon required a lot of background reading and study. I wanted to be as certain as possible about the validity of the phrase 'Long-term drugging with antipsychotics causes brain shrinkage.' My starting point was a book: *The Bitterest Pills* by Dr Joanna Moncrieff. From this I tracked down several research papers and journal articles on the subject. In the end, I was persuaded by the weight of evidence pointing to the inescapable conclusion: Antipsychotic drugs are Neurotoxic. That said, I can't help but admire the heroic strides of other experts in torturing the evidence to fit their preferred hypothesis: Antipsychotics are Neuroprotective.

It amazes me how clinicians and academics can spend their research careers designing studies and gathering evidence, only to stubbornly point their noses in entirely the wrong direction. They can't all be Shill Docs. Here's Joanna Moncrieff's take on this:

"It is as if the psychiatric community cannot bear to acknowledge its own published findings. Not only does the evidence on brain shrinkage have damning implications for antipsychotic drug treatment, it also weakens one of the strongest pillars of the case that schizophrenia is a brain disease." *(The Myth of the Chemical Cure, p. 110)*

Dr Moncrieff weighs her words carefully, but 'damning' evidence of severe brain damage caused by long-term use of antipsychotics has been stacking up for decades, and for all that time doctors have been freely twisting the evidence to make it more palatable. My own brief exposure to Haldol in the 1990s gave me forewarning to steer the hell clear of 'antipsychotics', but I might well grab them in a heartbeat at the approaching terror of all-out disintegration. Who knows? And there are those who take them willingly, without coercion, and many more who do not have the luxury of choice – people sectioned in hospital, or mandated by Community Treatment Order. We all deserve honesty.

I was never a big fan of 'Who Wants to be a Millionaire?' but the simplicity of the show's format appealed to me as a way to present the evidence for iatrogenic brain shrinkage in cartoon form. The arguments about brain shrinkage rage on amongst big-name clinicians and academics, and I urge you to seek them out yourself. If you do, just keep an eye open for where the funding comes from – it can be very revealing.

# Cartoon violence tickles me pink

I was a sensitive child, quick to pick up on any hint of playground bullying or build-up of tension that might lead to a fight. Real world violence troubled me greatly, and yet I couldn't get enough of those old-timey classic cartoons they aired in the 1970s. Tom and Jerry was a favourite, the non-stop violence tickled me pink, and the older I get the funnier it seems.

*'Sir Simon: Defender of the Faith'* is inspired by the Royal College of Psychiatrists anti-BASH campaign. BASH is an acronym: Badmouthing, Attitudes and Stigmatisation in Healthcare. Professor Sir Simon Wessely reveals his disquiet...

"Stigma surrounding psychiatry doesn't begin and end with the experiences of patients; doctors too experience stigmatisation – for deciding to become psychiatrists. This has to stop, and this campaign is going to do that."

Cartoon gold! I pictured Professor Sir Simon as a medieval knight in armour, all pumped up and straining to lead the battle charge. But then I read further:

"Students considering the possibility of becoming a psychiatrist are often put off their career choice by influential consultants in other specialties."

Not 'stigmatisation' so much as a good old fashioned inter-disciplinary spat. I had my angle – Tom and Jerry, of course. Or, rather, Spike (the beefy bulldog) and Tom. From there on in I had enormous fun developing the idea, largely by reliving old episodes of Spike and Tom squaring up against each other.

Professor Sir Simon genuinely believes that rivals from other medical specialties who say that 'Psychiatry is Pseudoscience' are guilty of 'bashing' his profession. No thoughts about whether there is any validity to the criticism, just an instant defensive response and cry of 'stigma.'

When it comes to 'bashing', Psychiatry surely knows a thing or two. I settled on the image of an ECT machine to symbolise how this branch of the medical profession flexes its muscles, but I needed a joke brand name to set it off. On researching the names of real ECT machines for inspiration, the first one I came across happened to be the **Siemens Konvulsator**. Yes, even spelled with a K. Satirising psychiatry is SO EASY!!

## Fat Whopper #10: Coercion and torture are things of the past

When I first started cartooning, I told myself that I would stay away from the topic of coercive ECT – the very thought of it blindsided me with a tornado of impotent fury, obliterating any chance of creative expression. But then, from the other side of the world, came news of an act of such brutal treatment at the hands of Psychiatry that I felt I had to find a way.

Garth Daniels was being subjected to degrading, systematic and sustained torment in defiance of International Law. Not even intervention by the UN Human Rights Council could make the psychiatrist budge. With a little help from the media, Garth's case became known around the world. Much to its credit, the Australian Broadcasting Corporation aired a penetrating report, exposing this shameful abuse of power in the name of Psychiatry... but where was the profession's public condemnation of this casual and unlawful cruelty by one of their own? Their silence spoke volumes.

## Rattling the cage

I tried to make them listen... I really did. In desperation, I reached out to Professor Sir Simon Wessely, president of the Royal College of Psychiatrists, urging him to comment publicly on the treatment of Garth Daniels. In due course I received this reply from the 'Public Information and Engagement Manager' based in the College's 'Strategic Communications Department'...

"I am responding on behalf of Professor Wessely and the College. The Royal College of Psychiatrists is the professional and educational body for psychiatrists in the United Kingdom. It is therefore not possible to comment on issues outside of our geographical area as the availability of mental health services, local legislation, and the types of treatments available is different in each country. We are only able to comment on psychiatric practice in the United Kingdom." (Excerpt. 9th March 2016)

Let Wisdom Guide.

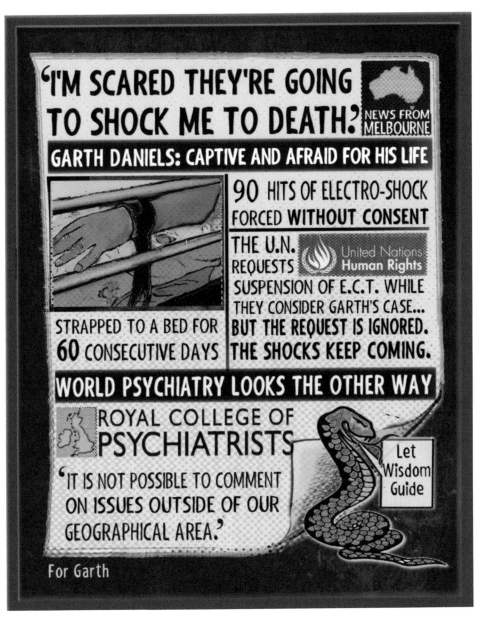

'I'M SCARED THEY'RE GOING TO SHOCK ME TO DEATH?

NEWS FROM MELBOURNE

GARTH DANIELS: CAPTIVE AND AFRAID FOR HIS LIFE

90 HITS OF ELECTRO-SHOCK FORCED WITHOUT CONSENT

THE U.N. REQUESTS SUSPENSION OF E.C.T. WHILE THEY CONSIDER GARTH'S CASE... BUT THE REQUEST IS IGNORED. THE SHOCKS KEEP COMING.

STRAPPED TO A BED FOR 60 CONSECUTIVE DAYS

United Nations Human Rights

WORLD PSYCHIATRY LOOKS THE OTHER WAY

ROYAL COLLEGE OF PSYCHIATRISTS

'IT IS NOT POSSIBLE TO COMMENT ON ISSUES OUTSIDE OF OUR GEOGRAPHICAL AREA.'

Let Wisdom Guide

For Garth

One of the expressions that sets my teeth on edge is this: 'I can't imagine...' as in 'I can't imagine what he must be going through'. The whole point of being human is that we *can* imagine. So, yes, you *can* imagine what it's like to be strapped to a bed for 60 days straight, you *can* imagine how it feels to be forcibly anaesthetized and convulsed with electro-shock 3 times a week, you *can* imagine pleading in vain for them to pause, to reconsider, to stop. You *can* imagine, you can, you can, you can.

## Fighting Talk

How do you fight in the face of such institutional complacency? Professor Sir Simon is ever-so willing to acknowledge the mistakes of his predecessors…

"It is also the sign of a mature profession, which is what I believe we are, that it does not shy away from, or turn a blind eye, to an uncomfortable past." *(The President's Blog, May 2016)*

…but where is his moral leadership in the 'uncomfortable' present? Further investigation reveals that his policy of refusing to comment on issues outside the UK is somewhat selective. May 2016 brought headline news from Holland:

"Sex abuse victim in her 20s allowed by doctors to choose euthanasia due to 'incurable' PTSD" *(Independent. 11th May 2016)*

And Professor Sir Simon had no qualms in tweeting…

"A lethal injection for a 20 yr old who suffered chronic sexual abuse & has ongoing mental illness? Feels so wrong."

Now, there's no doubt that this case is bristling with complex and thorny dilemmas for Psychiatry – not least their role in spreading the 'mental illness is an illness like any other' meme – but isn't the President of the Royal College of Psychiatrists supposed to keep mum?

Later in 2016, I gained insight into Prof Wessely's twisted take on ECT. What concerns him 'more than anything' is *public image.*

"We know that ECT has a small, though well-defined and sometimes life-saving role to play. But more than anything else when done badly it can give us a bad press that can take decades to overcome." *(The President's blog, October 2016.)*

So, of *course* I'm anti-psychiatry. Aren't you?

This is no joke. In a joint project, Proteus Digital Health and Otsuka Pharmaceuticals are designing drugs with embedded ingestible sensors. No surprise that Big Pharma has chosen blockbuster psych-drug Abilify to kick off the smart pill revolution – it is already being touted as a leap forward in ensuring that psychiatric patients 'adhere to treatment regimens'. Coercive drugging has never looked so sinister.

## Anosognosia: The self-reinforcing double bind

The notion of 'lack of insight' in Psychiatry is not new, but it has received a turbo-boost in recent years, largely due to the efforts of the influential Treatment Advocacy Center (TAC). The Greek word 'Anosognosia' has been co-opted from the field of Neurology, lending the concept an air of scientific credibility, which is further enhanced by TAC's emphatic insistence that Anosognosia is not just commonplace *denial...* it is *'caused by physical damage to the brain, and is thus anatomical in origin.'* Is there a differential diagnosis to distinguish the two? Of course not... it's psychiatry.

## Get out of this...

"Anosognosia is a reciprocating, self-reinforcing double bind. What should be terrifying to the public is how easy it is to get a label and impossible it is to disprove the label, once applied. At the moment, the public takes comfort in faith of a diagnosis, and treatment that at least doesn't make things worse. I'm sure the women executed for witchcraft in Salem had the same faith, up until the time they were accused." *(Marcellas Shale, www.anosognosiac.com)*

The TAC claims that Anosognosia is *'the single largest reason why people with schizophrenia or bipolar disorder refuse medications'.* So, imagine this: You have been diagnosed with schizophrenia, but the psych-drugs make you feel out of it and crappy and fuck up your head, so you refuse to take them. Here we go: 1) Your non-compliance is seen as evidence that you 'lack insight' into your illness. 2) You are 'diagnosed' with Anosognosia. 3) This diagnosis *proves* that you lack insight. 4) And this lack of insight accounts for your irrational non-compliance. Another case of warped circular logic. Psychiatry's solution? No prizes for guessing: *coercion.*

'An obvious solution to the nonadherence problem is to switch the individual from oral medication to long-acting injectable preparations' *(TAC Recommendations)*

So, of *course* I'm anti-psychiatry. Aren't you?

The patient in this cartoon is acutely aware that he must convince the doctor that he is 'ill' – the poster behind him spells out the consequences if he fails to do so. He cowers behind a façade, displaying to the doctor that he knows he's ill, yes siree! The façade is based on a mugshot of a prisoner, which is how the patient feels in that room. I added the caption 'A shared moment of insight' because the doctor looks like he may be having a lightbulb moment too… but I'm not sure what it might be.

# Afterword

This book is the culmination of three decades' study, exploration, personal struggle, connecting with like-minded people and generally noodling things over. It has been a quite a trek, but am I any closer to answering the question I set myself at the beginning of this book: "What does it mean to be anti-psychiatry?" I think Dr Henry Nasrallah may have the answer...

"Psychiatry is the only medical specialty with a long-time nemesis; it's called 'anti-psychiatry'." *(Current Psychiatry 2011 www.mdedge.com)*

Psychiatry's Nemesis. Oh please, oh please!

It is customary to provide a full list of references at the end of a book, but instead I have given pointers within the text to indicate where to find the source material. I hope you have the wherewithal to track these down. Over the years, certain books, papers and web resources have made a great impact and shaped my thinking – here are the ones that have had the biggest influence on this book:

**Peter Breggin:** *Toxic Psychiatry (1993)* The original and best.

**Joanna Moncrieff:** *Myth of the Chemical Cure (2008)* and *The Bitterest Pills (2013)*. Avidly read and heavily mined for quotes.

**Lucy Johnstone:** *Straight Talking Introduction to Psychiatric Diagnosis (2014)*. A shining gem of a book.

**Ethan Watters:** *Crazy Like Us: The Globalization of the Western Mind (2010)* A chilling picture of the world we've sleep-walked into.

**Philip Hickey:** *Website. Behaviorism and Mental Health.* Exposes the abuses and absurdities of Psychiatry like no-one else.

**Mad in America:** *Website.* An invaluable resource. Many of my cartoon ideas were sparked by blog posts to MiA.

**Robert Whitaker:** *Anatomy of an Epidemic (2011)*

## About the author

Auntie Psychiatry was born into a dairy farming family in Lancashire, England in 1969, the sixth of seven siblings. She graduated from University of Wales, Cardiff in 1990, obtaining a B.Sc. (Hons) in Pharmacology, and went on to research the side-effects of 'antipsychotic' drugs at Manchester University for a Master's degree, graduating in 1992. During this time, she began to question established Psychiatric theories and practice. She turned to cartooning in 2015 as a creative outlet for her growing sense of disquiet at the damage being done in the name of Psychiatry. Her biggest cartoonist influences are Gary Larson, Dr Seuss and Matt Groening. You can find her at: www.auntiepsychiatry.com

Printed in Poland
by Amazon Fulfillment
Poland Sp. z o.o., Wrocław